M000236190

GALE

CENGAGE Learning

Novels for Students, Volume 4 Copyright Notice

by all applicable copyright laws, as well as by misappropriation, trade secret, unfair competition, and other applicable laws. The authors and editors of this work have added value to the underlying factual material herein through one or more of the following: unique and original selection, coordination, expression, arrangement, and classification of the information. All rights to this publication will be vigorously defended.

Seize the Day

Saul Bellow

1956

Introduction

Bellow's fourth novel, *Seize the Day* was published as a novella in 1956 in a volume that also included three short stories—"A Father-to-Be," "Looking for Mr. Green," and "The Gonzaga Manuscripts"—and a play, *The Wrecker.* Considered by many critics to be Bellow's finest work of fiction, the novella was immediately singled out from among its companion pieces as a major work. The powerful impact of *Seize the Day* comes from its tightly constructed plot; from Bellow's ability to control effectively in a concentrated form such enormous themes as victimization, alienation, and human connection; and from his creation of Tommy Wilhelm, one of his most moving protagonists.

Bellow's work before *Seize the Day* had attracted the attention of readers and critics, but he was particularly praised for his achievement in this fourth novel, which Baker says "demonstrates his attainment of full artistic maturity." *Seize the Day* deals with themes familiar to readers of Bellow's fiction, such as that of the father-son relationship, yet in this novella the concentrated structure enabled Bellow to render this theme more intensely.

At the heart of the action in *Seize the Day*, Tommy Wilhelm's relationship with his father revolves around Tommy's neediness and his father's disapproval of him. Tommy's problems with his father feed yet another theme of the novel and of Bellow' s fiction in general: alienation from oneself and from humanity. Tommy feels cut off not only from his father and from the rest of his family—his sister, his dead mother, his estranged wife and their two sons—but he also feels alienated from himself and from everyone he meets. Bellow's ability to treat weighty themes in *Seize the Day*, while making Tommy Wilhelm a pitiable yet sympathetic character, explains the success of this novella: it is capable of seizing both the reader's mind and heart.

Author Biography

Saul Bellow is recognized as one of the most important American writers of the twentieth century. The youngest of four children, Bellow was born in 1915 to Russian immigrant parents in Lachine, Quebec, Canada, a suburb of Montreal. Bellow's father, Abraham, had come to Canada from Russia just two years before his youngest child was born. While living in Montreal, Bellow learned English, Hebrew, Yiddish, and French. He lived with his family in Montreal's Jewish ghetto until the family moved to Chicago when he was nine.

Bellow spent a great deal of time in libraries as a child, as he loved to read. His family struggled with financial difficulties during his youth. His father wanted Bellow to go into a lucrative profession such as law or medicine, and his mother wanted him to become a scholar of Jewish law and tradition. Instead, Bellow chose to study anthropology and sociology—the sciences of man and of society—and to become a writer and a teacher of writing. Bellow's writing came to reflect his chosen educational focus, as his work examines large themes such as the value of existence and the ways that people relate to each other.

While the themes he explores in his fiction are universal, Bellow's fiction is informed by his Russian and Jewish background and by his wide reading in American and European literature, as well as by his familiarity with the modern urban landscape. His heroes—Tommy Wilhelm, for example—are typically thinking men, Jewish urbandwellers who are in search of meaning in the world. Bellow himself, at the time he wrote *Seize the Day*, was interested in Reichianism, a sociological-psychological belief system based on the thought of Wilhelm Reich. According to Eusebio Rodrigues, Bellow's interest in Reichianism helped to shape *Seize the Day*.

Reichianism, says Rodrigues, revolves around the belief that human beings possess "a three-tiered character structure." The first tier consists of "man's natural sociality, his enjoyment of work, and his innate capacity for love"; the second tier consists of "inhibited drives of greed, lust, envy, and sadism"; and the "outer layer is a mask of politeness, self-control, and artificial sociality." Bellow has acknowledged that during the 1950s, when *Seize the Day* was published, he and a friend were involved in Reichianism, and Rodrigues proposes that "The three layers of Tommy Wilhelm are apparent as he lives through his tragic day."

Chapter I

Saul Bellow's *Seize the Day* is the story of one day in the life of Wilhelm Adler, a.k.a. Tommy Wilhelm, a man in his mid-forties who is going through a mid-life crisis. As the book opens he is standing outside of the dining room in the residential hotel in which he lives, contemplating his troubles and working up the courage to go in to breakfast and face his father, who also lives in the Gloriana Hotel.

Wilhelm reminisces about how he left school twenty-five years ago in order to go to Hollywood to try to become a movie star. He had at first been approached by a talent scout, Maurice Venice, but even after the screen test went badly and the scout tried to discourage him, Wilhelm decided to change his name to Tommy Wilhelm and go to California. Once there he discovered that Maurice Venice was himself a failure and that a recommendation from him was a curse.

He nevertheless stayed in Hollywood for seven years, unwillingly to admit defeat. Now, twenty-five years later, he finds himself unemployed, broke, and in despair. He is separated from his wife, but she refuses to give him a divorce. He has invested his last money in the commodities market, and he fears it is all lost. And he is endlessly quarreling with his father, who refuses to help Wilhelm and who seems to be ashamed of his son.

Chapter 2

Still working up the courage to face his father at breakfast, Wilhelm collects his mail. He has received a number of bills, including some from his wife, who wants him to pay the premiums on some educational insurance plans for their two boys. He finally goes into breakfast, where his father introduces him to an elderly man named Mr. Perls. They have a quarrelsome breakfast, with Dr. Adler feeling ashamed of his unemployed and slovenly son and Wilhelm resenting his father's unwillingness to help him in any way.

Dr. Adler presses his son to tell Mr. Perls about his former job as a salesman, which he lost after quarreling with his employers. Wilhelm is disgusted with how focused on money his father and Mr. Perls are. Dr. Adler and Mr. Perls begin discussing Dr. Tamkin, another resident of the hotel and the man to whom Wilhelm had trusted to invest his last seven hundred dollars in the commodities market. The two older men feel that Tamkin is a fraud and a fool, and as he listens to them, Wilhelm again begins to worry about his money.

Chapter 3

Mr. Perls leaves and Wilhelm and his father continue to argue. Wilhelm reveals how he tried to get a divorce so that he could marry another woman, Olive, but his wife continually refused to give him the divorce. Wilhelm recites many of his problems, but his father does not sympathize, feeling that everything is the result of Wilhelm's poor choices and not wanting to be burdened with caring for his adult children in his last few years. His parting advice to Wilhelm is "Carry nobody on your back."

Chapter 4

After leaving the dining room, Wilhelm seeks out Tamkin. They head to the commodities market to see how their stocks have done. Wilhelm spends the conversation trying to figure out whether Tamkin is trustworthy or not. They discuss many philosophical matters, and Wilhelm is attracted to the doctor's ideas, especially his philosophy about living in the present and seizing the day, but he is suspicious of Tamkin nonetheless.

Chapter 5

They arrive at the commodities market and take their place next to some friends of Tamkin. Wilhelm becomes nervous about the money, and when he sees that some of their shares have risen, he wants to sell and recover at least some of their lost money. Tamkin insists that they should leave their shares alone, and he says that Wilhelm needs to learn to trust and to live in the here and now. As Tamkin tries to show him some methods for focusing on the here and now, Wilhelm wonders if the doctor is trying to hypnotize or con him.

Chapter 6

They go to lunch and discuss Wilhelm's problems with his wife and father. Wilhelm realizes that although Tamkin is probably a charlatan, he also believes that Tamkin has managed to survive for a long time, and he hopes that perhaps he can help him to survive as well. He begins to feel that he is "on Tamkin's back," trusting the other man to take the necessary steps for him.

They return to the commodities market, but before they can enter Mr. Rappaport, a very old man who was sitting next to them earlier, greets them. He demands that Wilhelm take him to the cigar store, and when Wilhelm protests that he wants to check on his commodities, Tamkin pushes him to go with Rappaport, insisting that he can learn a lot from the elderly man. When he returns from the cigar store Wilhelm finds that his commodities have dropped so far that he has lost all of his money. Tamkin is nowhere to be found.

Chapter 7

Wilhelm comes to the painful realization that it was he that had been carrying Tamkin on his back. He goes to his father to ask for help, but his father refuses him, yelling at him and telling him that he will not support his grown children. Wilhelm reminds him that there are other things besides money that a father can give a son, but his father refuses to listen. He says that he will see Wilhelm dead before he will allow his son to become a cross for him to bear.

Wilhelm goes in search of Tamkin. He receives an urgent message from his wife. Fearing that something has happened to one of his boys, he calls her. She is angry that he has sent her a post-dated check. They quarrel, and she blames him for the separation and for his unemployment. He resolves that he will find Tamkin and at least recover the two hundred dollars that the doctor owed him. He hopes that he will be able to start again with Olive, the woman he wanted to marry.

Searching for Tamkin he comes across a funeral procession, and he thinks that he sees Tamkin in the crowd. As he tries to get closer, he is swept into the church and eventually finds himself looking at the dead man in the casket. He is overwhelmed by grief at the death of the stranger. He sobs uncontrollably, and the other mourners wonder who he is and how he knew the deceased. Wilhelm only continues to sob.

Characters

Dr. Adler

Tommy Wilhelm's elderly father, Dr. Adler lives at the Hotel Gloriana in New York but "in an entirely different world from his son." Wilhelm's relationship with his father is at the center of the novel. Dr. Adler is a handsome, orderly, well-dressed man who is respected by all who know him. He has retired from his medical practice and is financially secure, but he refuses to lend money to his son, whom he continues to call by his childhood name, "Wilky." Tommy/Wilky disgusts Dr. Adler in his sloppiness, his emotional intensity, and his seeming inability to make a good decision, and Dr. Adler is impatient with his son's apparent lack of initiative.

When he talks about his son to friends and acquaintances, Dr. Adler builds up Wilky's achievements in an attempt to impress his listeners, although in truth he is not proud of his son. Although Tommy/Wilky pleads with his father to care for him—"'I expect *help!*'"—Dr. Adler is unmoved. He tells his son that if he were to help him by giving him money to cover his bills, it would only make Tommy/Wilky dependent on him. He also refuses to help his daughter, who also wants his financial assistance, explaining himself by declaring "'I want nobody on my back. Get off!'"

Catherine

Wilhelm's younger sister, Catherine has taken "a professional name," Philippa. She is a painter and has asked Dr. Adler for money to rent a gallery for an exhibition of her work, but he refuses to support her. Neither Wilhelm nor his father thinks Catherine has talent.

Dad

See Dr. Adler

Father

See Dr. Adler

Margaret

Margaret is Tommy Wilhelm's estranged wife, whom he claims is "'killing'" him by constantly demanding money from him. Margaret will not divorce Wilhelm, and because she is raising their two boys, she refuses to get a job. Tommy sees Margaret as "unbending, remorselessly unbending."

Olive

Wilhelm's girlfriend in Roxbury, whom he used to see when he was working for the Rojax Corporation. He wanted to marry her, but their marriage was prevented by Margaret's refusal to divorce Wilhelm.

Paul

Tommy Wilhelm's younger son, Paul, is "going to be ten." He calls his father a "'hummuspotamus,'" or hippopotamus.

Media Adaptations

- *Seize the Day* was adapted in 1986 as a film featuring Robin Williams, Joseph Wiseman, Jerry Stiller, and Glenne Headly, and with a cameo appearance by Bellow; this film aired on PBS in 1987. Directed by Fielder Cook; available on VHS and Laserdisc; distributed by HBO (Canada).

Mr. Perls

Another elderly resident of the Hotel Gloriana and a friend of Dr. Adler's, Mr. Perls is introduced to Wilhelm as having been a "hosiery wholesaler," but Wilhelm perceives from his appearance that he has had a difficult life. His presence at breakfast annoys Wilhelm: he sees Perls as his father's way of avoiding being alone with him. Wilhelm also despises his father's need to impress Perls by boasting about his children's accomplishments, particularly because neither one has been especially successful. Perls is eager to know the details of Wilhelm's salary and position at the Rojax Corporation, and Wilhelm is disgusted by his intense interest in money.

Philippa

See Catherine

Mr. Rappaport

Rappaport is the blind old retired chicken merchant whom Wilhelm sits near in the brokerage office. Wilhelm envies Rappaport's ability to remain calm about the fluctuating stock market; he does not have as much to lose as Wilhelm does. As Wilhelm returns to the brokerage office after leaving for lunch, Rappaport meets him outside and asks him to take him across the street to the cigar store. Wilhelm reluctantly agrees, as this errand delays his return to the market. When he does return, he learns he is ruined.

Mr. Rowland

Wilhelm sits near Mr. Rowland in the brokerage office as they watch the progress of their stocks. According to Tamkin, Rowland supports himself on his earnings from the stock market. This fact gives Wilhelm hope as he invests his last few hundred dollars.

Rubin

The well-dressed Rubin is "the man at the newsstand" in the Hotel Gloriana where Tommy Wilhelm lives. Wilhelm thinks of Rubin as "the kind of man who knew, and knew and knew."

Dr. Tamkin

The mysterious Dr. Tamkin claims to be a psychologist but turns out to be a con artist: he tricks Tommy Wilhelm into giving him his last seven hundred dollars to invest while assuring Tommy that this investment will make him wealthy. Tamkin, like Wilhelm and Dr. Adler, lives at the Hotel Gloriana, and the men know each other through a nightly card game. Wilhelm's father calls Tamkin "'cunning … an operator,'" but Wilhelm wants to believe that Tamkin can make him rich, so he makes himself trust this man with "a hypnotic power in his eyes."

Tamkin tells Wilhelm incredible stories about his work with his patients and insists that "'I have to do good wherever I can.'" He presents to Wilhelm his belief that in each human being "'there are two main [souls], the real soul and a pretender soul.'" Essentially, he is speaking about alienation from oneself, a subject that resonates with Wilhelm. In spite of his philosophical revelations, Tamkin remains a mystery to Wilhelm, who never quite comes to trust him fully. When Wilhelm realizes he has been ruined on the stock market and can't find Tamkin, who has slipped away from the brokerage office, Wilhelm is not completely surprised to understand at last that Tamkin is a fake.

Tommy

Tommy is Tommy Wilhelm's 14-year-old son, the older of his two boys.

Maurice Venice

Maurice Venice is the shady talent scout who approached the handsome young Wilhelm Adler—now Tommy Wilhelm—with the idea that he should go out to Hollywood to try to become a star. Wilhelm had a warning sense that Venice "protested too much" about his credentials. Yet he made his "first great mistake" by giving in to Venice's pressure, abandoning college, and going to Hollywood only to find when he got there that "a recommendation from Maurice Venice was the kiss of death."

Tommy Wilhelm

Middle-aged, overweight, slovenly, out of work, estranged from his wife and arguing with his father, Tommy Wilhelm is the protagonist of Bellow's novel. Emotional rather than rational, Wilhelm tends to make bad decisions. On the day portrayed in the novel, he is feeling as though all of his bad decisions are coming together to choke him; he repeatedly says things like "'I just can't catch my breath'" and that he feels "congested" and "'about to burst.'" In addition to being on the verge of financial ruin, Wilhelm feels alone in the world. He has left his wife and their two sons, although his wife will not give him a divorce and he misses his sons terribly. He is estranged from his mistress, Olive. He does not see his only sister, his mother died years ago, and although he and his father live "'under the same roof' " of the Hotel Gloriana, his father does not approve of him.

Wilhelm's conversations with his father center on Wilhelm's need for "'help,'" but while his father, Dr. Adler, interprets his pleas for help as being merely financial, Wilhelm also is asking for his father's approval and some kindness. Wilhelm is, however, down to his last few dollars and is extremely self-conscious about his lack of money. He feels bitterly that the world has "a sort of hugging relish" for money: "Everyone was supposed to have money.... They'd be ashamed not to have it." Wilhelm's inner confusion is represented in part by his confusion over which name is his true name: Wilky, his childhood name; Tommy Wilhelm, the name he chooses when he goes to Hollywod; or Velvel, the Yiddish name his old grandfather had called him.

Wilky

See Tommy Wilhelm

Themes

Alienation and Loneliness

Tommy Wilhelm's sense of estrangement not only from his own family but also from his acquaintances and the entire city of New York places the themes of alienation and loneliness at the core of the novel. From the novel's opening scene, in which Wilhelm talks briefly with "Rubin, the man at the newsstand," it is clear that these men know many things about each other, and yet "None of these could be mentioned, and the great weight of the unspoken left them little to talk about."

Wilhelm longs to connect on an emotional level with his father, but old Dr. Adler speaks to his son "with such detachment about his welfare" that Wilhelm, Adler's "one and only son, could not speak his mind or ease his heart to him." Wilhelm's sense of alienation from himself is represented by his confusion over his different names: his father calls him "Wilky," his childhood name, but Wilhelm had chosen the name "Tommy Wilhelm," dropping the name Adler, when he went to Hollywood to pursue an acting career.

When Dr. Tamkin talks to Wilhelm about his ideas on the soul, Wilhelm recognizes himself in Tamkin's description of "two main [souls], the real soul and a pretender soul." Wilhelm is "awed" by Tamkin's vision: "In Tommy he saw the pretender.

And even Wilky might not be himself. Might the name of his true soul be the one by which his old grandfather had called him—Velvel?"

Looking outside of himself and his small circle, Wilhelm feels alienated from humanity, as represented by New York City and its inhabitants. He feels that communication with others is as difficult as learning another language: "Every other man spoke a language entirely his own, which he had figured out by private thinking … and this happened over and over and over with everyone you met. You had to translate and translate, explain and explain, back and forth, and it was the punishment of hell itself not to understand or be understood...." Wilhelm has a encompassing sense that the alienation he feels is not unique to him, but that "everybody is outcast," that the experience of loneliness is part of the human condition.

Topics for Further Study

- Research middle-class marriage in the 1950s. What roles were married men and women expected to play, and how successful was this model?

- Investigate post-World War II trends in popular psychology and self-help literature. Based on the popularity of the literature you find, can you speculate as to the kinds of advice and support Americans were looking for? What might these needs tell us about American culture at the time?

- During the years of President Eisenhower's terms of office—1952 to 1960—what was the general view of success among the middle-class? What did it mean to be successful in 1950s America?

American Dream

The so-called "American Dream" has taken many shapes—streets paved with gold, a chicken in every pot—but the theme is always the same: financial success. Bellow looks at a dark side of this dream—what happens when a believer in the American Dream fails to succeed? Tommy Wilhelm feels the pressure of the American Dream. Money, or the lack of it, is an irritant to Wilhelm. His success as a salesman for the Rojax Corporation is in the past, and "Now he had to rethink the future, because of the money problem."

Wilhelm's "money problem" is that he no longer has any—he has given his last seven hundred dollars to the dubious Tamkin to invest in stocks, but in the meantime he cannot pay this month's rent, nor does he have any money to send to his estranged wife to support her and their two sons. Wilhelm looks around him and sees everywhere the expectation that he should have money: "Holy money! Beautiful money! ... if you didn't have it you were a dummy, a dummy! You had to excuse yourself from the face of the earth."

Wilhelm's lack of income and his anxiety about his precarious position clearly influence his attitude about money and the American Dream. Part of this Dream is that one's children should find more success in the world than one has found, and Wilhelm is highly aware that his father, a respected doctor, amassed more wealth than Wilhelm himself will ever be able to do.

Father and Son

Wilhelm's sense of disconnection from the world seems to start with his relationship with his father. When Wilhelm tells Tamkin about his struggles with his father, Tamkin comments, "'It's the eternal same story ... The elemental conflict of parent and child. It won't end, ever.'"

The theme of father and son appears in much of Bellow's fiction, and in *Seize the Day* it drives much of the plot. Wilhelm, or Wilky, as his father calls him, cannot satisfy his father, and his father refuses to help Wilhelm. "'My dad is something of a stranger to me,'" Wilhelm tells Tamkin, although he admits, "'of course I love him.'" When Wilhelm asks his father for help, Dr. Adler refuses "'to take on new burdens,'" but Wilhelm replies, "'it isn't all a question of money—there are other things a father can give a son.'" He pleads with Dr. Adler, "'I expect *help!*'" but Dr. Adler seems incapable of giving the kind of help his son needs.

Individual vs. Society

A teeming, confusing New York City provides an appropriate setting for Tommy Wilhelm's overwhelming day of alienation and ruin. Wilhelm sees himself as an outsider in his world. Although he was born and raised in this city, Wilhelm feels like a stranger here: "I don't belong in New York any more." New York takes on an apocalyptic quality for Wilhelm when he thinks about the failure of communication in such a place: "New York—the end of the world, with its complexity and machinery, bricks and tubes, wires and stones, holes and heights. And was everybody crazy here?"

Wilhelm's deepest need is for connection, for the sympathetic understanding of another person. He feels completely alone in a city that seems to assault him: "'There's too much push for me here. It works me up too much.'" He does have one transcendental moment of connection with humanity—a "blaze of love"—while passing through an underground corridor beneath Times Square: "... all of a sudden, unsought, a general love for all these imperfect and lurid-looking people burst out in Wilhelm's breast. He loved them. One and all, he passionately loved them. They were his brothers and sisters."

But this romantically sweeping sense of connection does not last and in retrospect seems to Wilhelm to have been an arbitrary event, "only another one of those subway things. Like having a hard-on at random." Finally, in the last moments of the novel, when Wilhelm weeps in a funeral parlor over the corpse of a stranger, he is able to move "toward the consummation of his heart's ultimate need" when he recognizes that mortality is the bond among human beings.

Success and Failure

Tommy Wilhelm has made a series of mistakes and bad decisions in his life, and "through such decisions somehow his life had taken form." Motivated by feeling or emotion rather than by rational thought, Wilhelm decided to go to Hollywood to try to become a "screen artist," to leave the Rojax Corporation because his territory was being divided and he was not being promoted, and to give Tamkin the last of his money. All of these decisions, made in hopes of finding some kind of success, have resulted in Wilhelm's failure. He ponders the fact that in the past "He had been slow to mature, and he had lost ground." At the nightly gin game in which he often participates, Wilhelm "had never won. Not once…. He was tired of losing."

His father, in order to preserve appearances to his friends, emphasizes Wilhelm's past success as a salesman with the Rojax Corporation when he introduces his son, but this emphasis on the past only serves to highlight what a failure Wilhelm is now. Wilhelm's father, Dr. Adler, is considered a success, not only in terms of his financial attainment or his achievements in his field prior to his retirement, but also in terms of his character: "He was idolized by everyone." In contrast to his son, Dr. Adler is controlled and self-contained and is not ruled by his emotions but is instead rational. Wilhelm's failure is connected to his lack of control and "style," while his father's success stems from his restraint and his ability to master appearances.

Point of View

The third-person, limited omniscient point of view in *Seize the Day* provides a balanced view of the actions of the characters while offering some insight into the protagonist's mind. Thus Wilhelm is the central consciousness of the novel without being the narrator. The point of view of the novel recreates Wilhelm's frantic, disorderly state of mind while placing Wilhelm amongst his more orderly father and the rational Tamkin. A first-person narration by Wilhelm would prevent a balanced view of his father and other characters, as the world of the novel would be shaped by Wilhelm's internal turmoil. Yet a third-person narration that also accounts for Wilhelm's thoughts enables a controlled sequence of events while creating for sympathy for the protagonist.

Setting

New York City plays a crucial role as the setting for *Seize the Day*. The city itself, huge and teeming with infinite forms of activity, serves as a backdrop to Wilhelm's confusion and sense of isolation, but it also inhabits Wilhelm's imagination as a force that presses upon his soul and chokes him. The swarming sidewalks of New York help to create Wilhelm's sense that communication with others is impossible: he sees there "the great, great crowd, the inexhaustible current of millions of every race and kind pouring out, pressing round, of every age, of every genius, possessors of every human secret ... in every face the refinement of one particular motive or essence." Wilhelm feels out of place in the city and prefers the country, his memories of which soothe his mind.

Wilhelm's home in the city, a rented room at The Hotel Gloriana, reflects his transient status in New York. In addition, "most of the guests at the Hotel ... were past the age of retirement," and "a great part of New York's vast population of old men and women" lives in the neighborhood of the hotel. Thus Wilhelm, only forty-four himself, is living like an elderly person, which is indicative of his sense that his life is essentially over.

Images/Imagery

Images of water and drowning permeate *Seize the Day*, reflecting Wilhelm's feeling that he is choking and suffocating. From the opening paragraph, in which Wilhelm rides the elevator that "sank and sank," and eventually reaches the lobby where the carpet "billowed toward [his] feet," Bellow presents a series of images that suggest water and its potential threat. Wilhelm's father presses his son to stop taking so many pills and to try hydrotherapy—"'Simple water has a calming effect'"—but Wilhelm's response is "'I thought ... that the water cure was for lunatics.'"

Wilhelm connects images of death by water with his sense of personal ruin: "The waters of the earth are going to roll over me." Ominously, Tamkin tells Wilhelm that his wife drowned, a suspected suicide, and Tamkin insists that for Wilhelm to understand the process of investing he had to take a risk: "'To know how it feels to be a seaweed you have to get in the water.'" In the final moments of the novel, as Wilhelm is overwhelmed by emotion at the funeral of a stranger, he hears the "heavy, sea-like music" and "[sinks] deeper than sorrow," seemingly about to drown in his own tears.

Anti-hero

While a hero is traditionally a fortunate individual of superhuman power or spirit, an anti-hero is by definition the opposite of a hero and is thus a person who is neither strong nor purposeful. An anti-hero may be portrayed as having little control over events, seeming aimless or confused, or as being out of step with society. Tommy Wilhelm is an anti-hero. He seems to drift through his life, making poor decisions that remove him farther and farther from his family and friends, and he feels like an outsider in the city of his birth. He is down on his luck in *Seize the Day*, but his bad luck is connected to the "great mistakes" he has made throughout his life.

Catharsis

Catharsis is a release of built-up emotion, and

the classical definition of catharsis involves a combination of terror and pity in that release. As the images of Wilhelm's growing frustration and desperation mount, the novel creates a sense that something has to give before Wilhelm, in his own words, "bursts" or "chokes." In the final moments of the novel, the realization of his utter financial ruin dawns upon Wilhelm. He sees at the same time that Tamkin, whom he had trusted and had looked up to as a kind of spiritual advisor, has betrayed his trust. Thus two main threads of the novel—Wilhelm's fears about his financial instability and his intense desire for human connection—have simultaneously and devastatingly come to a head.

As Wilhelm goes into the street, blindly searching for Tamkin, he goes into a funeral parlor, where he suddenly finds himself beside the coffin of a stranger. In Wilhelm's thoughts as he gazes upon the corpse's face—"A man—another human creature ... What'll I do? I'm stripped and kicked out.... Oh, Father, what do I ask of you? What'll I do about the kids—Tommy, Paul? My children"—all of his fears and feelings of isolation coalesce. He breaks down, "past words, past reason, past coherence.... The source of all tears had suddenly sprung open within him." This moment, when Wilhelm sinks "deeper than sorrow" and cries "with all his heart" is the catharsis of the novel.

Middle-Class Family Life and Suburbia in the 1950s

In the wake of World War II, middle-class life in the 1950s was relatively peaceful, though it was dominated by cultural expectations. Middle-class Americans were marrying younger and in greater numbers than previously, and many of these young married couples were moving out of the cities, building houses in the rapidly-expanding suburbs, and filling their new houses with babies. In most cases, the husband went into the city to work and the wife stayed home and took care of the house and the children.

Levittowns, developer William J. Levitt's huge suburbs on Long Island and in Pennsylvania, offered uniform houses on tiny lots and became enormously popular. Other developers imitated Levitt's mass-production methods in hopes of cashing in on the appeal of such suburbs. This appeal came from the promise of a quiet, safe life outside of the noisy cities, a life where one could belong to a community of others like oneself. Conformity in the suburbs was considered the norm. The suburbs of the 1950s were almost exclusively inhabited by whites. Many suburbs dictated that their residents could not change their yards or the exterior of their houses outside of stated parameters.

Rarely did elderly, single, homosexual, or childless couples buy homes in these new suburbs: the young white family dominated the scene. The development of the suburbs also fed the automobile industry, as living in the suburbs necessitated owning a car, and public transportation became much less popular than it had been.

Away from the movie houses of the cities, families living in the suburbs watched television for entertainment. At the beginning of the decade, television was far from being the ubiquitous presence it quickly became. But television grew immensely popular in the 1950s, as more and more middle-class consumers purchased their own TV sets. Popular shows included "I Love Lucy," "Father Knows Best," "The Untouchables," and "Gunsmoke," which today's audiences can still watch in syndication.

Fear in the 1950s

Fear of communists occupied the American imagination of the 1950s. During this post-World War II decade, anti-communism grew out of a fear of Soviet aggression and led many Americans to point accusing fingers at one another. One of the most notorious finger pointers was Senator Joseph McCarthy, whose systematic pursuit of communists in American society seized the country's attention for the first half of the decade.

From early 1950 to late 1954, McCarthy and his movement—dubbed "McCarthyism"—named government officials, authors and journalists, movie actors and directors, and many others, for the stated purpose of rooting out communism in American culture. Being named by McCarthy ruined many a career during the 1950s; for instance, actors were blacklisted and could not get work after being accused of communist practices. McCarthy was extremely popular; to a nation gripped by fear, he was a powerful figure. Although McCarthy did not invent anti-communism and in fact shared the anti-communist watch with many others, he remains a symbol of the hysteria and slander that characterized anti-communism in the 1950s.

Compare & Contrast

- **1950s:** In spite of a generally positive attitude toward capitalism, American participation in the stock market was not widespread, with stock owned by just 3.5 percent of working Americans in 1956.
  Today: Through Individual Retirement Accounts, mutual funds, and retirement plans, more Americans than ever before have money invested in the stock market.

- **1950s:** America popular culture—television shows, movies, magazines—portrayed marriage as essential to happiness, and within marriage, sex roles were strictly defined, with the husband as breadwinner and the wife as housekeeper and mother. Divorce among middle-class marriages was uncommon and considered a failure.

Today: Middle-class marriage and family life in America depend less upon cultural expectations and more upon what works for the individual family. Many middle-class married women work outside the home, divorce has become more common and accepted, and married couples often share housework, childcare, and other domestic duties.

- **1950s:** Because of the military, political, and economic triumphs of the 1940s, the U.S. experienced unprecedented prosperity in the 1950s that led Americans to believe that affluence and middle-class status were a birthright.

  Today: Many middle-class American families need more than one income just to make ends meet.

- **1950s:** Norman Vincent Peale published his best-seller *The Power of Positive Thinking* in 1952, promoting a way of thinking that he assured readers would give them "peace of mind, improved health, and a never-ceasing flow of energy" and would help them "modify or change the circumstances in which [they] now live, assuming control over them rather than continuing to be directed by them."

Today: Best-selling authors like Stephen Covey *(Seven Habits of Highly Effective People)* and Richard Carlson *(Don't Sweat the Small Stuff* and *Don't Worry, Make Money)* claim to teach readers how to gain more satisfaction from their lives.

Related to the fear of communists and communism was the dread of nuclear warfare in the 1950s. The bombing of Hiroshima and Nagasaki in 1945 had shown the world the destructiveness of nuclear weapons, and this knowledge, combined with widespread fear of the Soviet Union, left Americans in constant fear of being bombed. Many Americans chose to build atomic bomb shelters—underground rooms outfitted with supplies—in case of nuclear attack, and schoolchildren were drilled in what to do if a bomb were dropped on their cities. Such drills included such ineffective strategies as "duck and cover," which required children to hide under their desks and cover their heads at the first warning of a nuclear attack. Living under the constant threat of the bomb created a sense of impending doom, but also a desire to pretend that everything is all right.

Critical Overview

When *Seize the Day* was published in 1956, critics praised the novella and maintained that it followed in a natural progression from Bellow's first three novels, *Dangling Man* (1944), *The Victim* (1947), and *The Adventures of Augie March* (1954). In his 1957 *Chicago Review* assessment of *Seize the Day*, Robert Baker wrote that Bellow in all of his novels "has tried to lasso the universe, to explore the splendid, profligate diversity of human experience, and to seek the ties that bind." Baker found that in *Seize the Day*, Bellow had matured as an artist: "The growth and ripening of Bellow's attitudes have been paralleled by the perfecting of his medium of expression."

Baker alluded in his review to the three short stories that accompany *Seize the Day* in the volume entitled *Seize the Day*, but he claimed that "these stories do not match the brilliance of 'Seize the Day,' and so the less said about them the better." Baker suggested that Bellow's writing does contain flaws, particularly that he fails to "deal convincingly with women" and that "his books don't end, they just stop." However, he called Bellow "perhaps the major talent of the past decade."

Irving Malin joined Baker in his praise *of Seize the Day*. In Malin's 1969 book *Saul Bellow's Fiction*, Malin called *Seize the Day* a "'blest nouvelle,'" or blessed novel. He asserted in his book, a study of Bellow's fiction through *Herzog* (1964), that *Seize the Day* was "Bellow's greatest achievement." Harry T. Moore, in his preface to Malin's book, called *Seize the Day* and *The Victim* "two of the finest novels to come out of America since World War II." Malin's assessment of Bellow in general was that he was "probably the most important living American novelist"; Malin's judgment was based on his belief that Bellow's work was "mature, human, [and] imaginative."

Robert R. Dutton in his book *Saul Bellow* (1971) discussed *Seize the Day* mainly in terms of the theme of the novel's sources, the father-son relationship between Tommy Wilhelm and Dr. Adler, Dr. Tamkin as a "Contemporary Witch-doctor," and the novel's water and drowning imagery. Although Dutton acknowledged that it is difficult for critics to make "definitive judgments" about contemporary American literature, he admitted that "Bellow's novels represent the contemporary American novel at its best," adding that this judgment came not only from literary critics but also from more popular sources such as newspaper book reviews and weekly news magazines. In attempting to make a distinction between Bellow and his fellow American novelists, Dutton asserted that "In each of [Bellow's] novels he finds the human spirit to be quietly triumphant, quietly able to sustain itself in an alien and unfriendly world."

Superlatives have often been used to describe Bellow's work. Brigitte Scheer-Schazler in her 1972 study of Bellow's fiction, *Saul Bellow*, devoted her introduction in part to discussing Bellow's critical reputation. She describes him as "America's most important living novelist," "a 'contemporary classic,'" and asserts that "no contemporary American novelist equals Bellow in the precision, wit, and elegance of his style." Scheer-Schazler noted that *Seize the Day* "contains elements that are familiar from former works." She focused on "the open and closed forms of Bellow's novels and his vacillating between tight and loose modes of language," placing *Seize the Day* in what she called the "'restrained' category." This tension in Bellow's fiction between what Scheer-Schazler called "emotional intensity" and "artistic control" represents "two diverging aspects of his talent."

In his introduction to *Critical Essays on Saul Bellow* (1979), which he edited, Stanley Trachtenberg wrote that in the early part of his career "Bellow reflected the interests of a new generation" that had come of age during the Depression and World War II. Trachtenberg saw Bellow as having "abandoned the ironic mode of alienation adopted by the modernists in favor of a moral judgment that emerged from the attempt to allow ideas a dramatic expression." In other words, Trachtenberg suggested, Bellow examined "the look and feel of things" in order to "establish the importance of action."

Eusebio Rodrigues nodded to the philosophical underpinnings of *Seize the Day* in his 1979 article "Reichianism in *Seize the Day.*" In this article,

Rodrigues discussed Bellow's early interest in the thought of Wilhelm Reich, "who combined the insights of a sociologist with those of a psychologist, [insisting] ... that the vast majority of human beings suffer from ... inner tensions generated by the conflict between natural human demands and the brutal pressures exerted by the world." Rodrigues stated that in *Seize the Day*, "Tommy Wilhelm is a dramatic illustration of how human character structure is molded and distorted by a society that is patriarchal, death-dealing, money-oriented and barren."

Sources

Robert Baker, "Bellow Comes of Age," in *Chicago Review*, Vol. 11, 1957, pp. 107-10.

Robert R. Dutton, *Saul Bellow*, Twayne Publishers, Inc., 1971.

Irving Malin, *Saul Bellow's Fiction*, Southern Illinois University Press, 1969.

Harry T. Moore, "Preface," in *Saul Bellow's Fiction* by Irving Malin, Southern Illinois Press, 1969.

Eusebio Rodrigues, "Reichianism in *Seize the Day,"* in *Critical Essays on Saul Bellow*, edited by Stanley Trachtenberg, G.K. Hall & Co., 1979, pp. 89-100.

Brigitte Scheer-Schazler, *Saul Bellow*, Frederick Ungar Publishing Co., 1972.

Stanley Trachtenberg, "Introduction," in *Critical Essays on Saul Bellow*, G.K. Hall & Co., 1979.

For Further Study

Robert Baker, a review in *Chicago Review*, Vol. 11, 1957, pp. 107-10.

> Asserts that *Seize the Day* demonstrates that Bellow has attained "full artistic maturity."

Richard Giannone, "Saul Bellow's Idea of Self: A Reading of *Seize the Day*," in *Renascence: Essays on Value in Literature*, Vol. 27, 1975, pp. 193-205.

> Sees Wilhelm, like all of Bellow's protagonists, on a quest to discover what makes him human and gives him dignity.

Andrew Jefchak, "Family Struggles in *Seize the Day*,'" in *Studies in Short Fiction*, Vol. 11, 1974, pp. 297-302.

> An analysis of the frustrated family relations in the novel and the alienation that results.

M. A. Klug, "Saul Bellow: The Hero in the Middle," in *Dalhousie Review*, Vol. 56, 1976, pp. 462-78.

> Views Bellow's work within the tradition of American literature and discusses his heroes from Joseph in *Dangling Man* through Sammler in *Mr. Sammler's Planet*. Klug believes

Bellow "offers the most sustained and penetrating criticism of contemporary American life of any novelist of his generation."

Julius Rowan Raper, "The Limits of Change: Saul Bellow's *Seize the Day* and *Henderson the Rain King*, " in *Narcissus from Rubble: Competing Models of Character in Contemporary British and American Fiction*, Louisiana State University Press, 1992, pp. 12-36.

According to Raper, Bellow's novels illustrate the fact that one can only change one's state and find one's self by discovering and relying on one's inner resources.

Lee J. Richmond, "The Maladroit, the Medico, and the Magician," in *Twentieth Century Literature*, Vol. 19, 1973, pp. 15-26.

Richmond perceives Dr. Tamkin as "the nexus for the novel's artistic truth."

Philip Stevick, "The Rhetoric of Bellow's Short Fiction," in *Critical Essays on Saul Bellow*, edited by Stanley Trachtenberg, G.K. Hall & Co., 1979, pp. 73-82.

Examining Bellow's short stories, including the three stories published along with *Seize the Day* in its first edition, Stevick discusses the "uncommon power and integrity" of

Bellow's short fiction.

CPSIA information can be obtained
at www.ICGtesting.com
Printed in the USA
BVHW040111050621
608823BV00014B/4011

9 781375 398923